THE LONG PLACE

THE LONG PLACE

LUIS MONTAÑO

ISBN: 978-0-692-45421-3

Printed in the United States of America

This book is printed on acid free, environmentally friendly FSC certified paper derived
entirely from renewable resources.

CONTENTS

Inscription on a stone slab seen upon leaving the Sala Azteca at Moseo Nacional de Antropologia, Mexico City, D.F.

Haz algo! Parte leña, labra la tierra, siembra maguey, levanta cercos. Con esto tendras que comer, conesto tendras que bever, con esto tendras de vestir. Con esto seras recto, con esto hablaran bien de ti. Los antecendientes no llegaron aqui de avarientos; ellos llegaron aqui como aguilas, como jaguares.

Act! Do something! Chop wood, work the soil, plant maguey, build fences. With this you shall have to eat, with this you shall have to drink, with this you will have clothes, with this you shall stand straight, with this they will speak well of you. Our elders did not come here to be greedy or selfish; they came here as eagles and jaguars

GRANIZAL

Plains lightning wrought this place.
Drops like tasteless blood,
seared meat down to the sinews,
sweet mesquite beans–thorns and all–
wrought this place.

All the old energies ring here.
The red silt sleeps in beds
where lightning struck
ten thousand years ago
and scared the deer.
Their fear made a pattern
of scurrilous light like ten synapses,
some bucks, some does.

Smelling like only wet deer smell, I come here.
Smelling like only struck flint smells, I come.
Sage crushed by hail hushes me to a sigh.

This ledge of stone gives much to pause for
as I peek from leaves
of wet scrub oak, sage, *manzanillo*.

All my life I'll be from here.
My heart belongs to that row
of goats pecked into the black
patinaed sandstone.
Belongs to the shards
that once contained this rain.

Out here is the blue haze
where thunder goes to when it's done
grinding air to ozone, so the *Dormilones*–
the evening boomerangs–can hang
and zoom, and give us peace as the sun sets.

BIRTHPLACE

On the mesa, above the red talus
the snow lies facing south,
smelling like clean sheets
on the clothesline.

Below are the last rocks
of the house where I was born
and the *acequia* where they buried
the placenta in some old repeated rite.

In this place, pure snows
caress the common grit,
and in the thaw,
the red clay bleeds through
like the sheets on the birthing bed . . .
it is March.

It Took a Day to Get to Anton Chico

My brothers and sisters send me pictures of food.
We trade pictures of *creciente* and giant pumpkins.
I still have the tough old negatives from
when it took a day's ride to Anton Chico.

That black bridge was already old when my uncles
stood me like a bowling pin in those hay fields.
Old when the Brownie Box with a five cent lens brought
a million squinting kids into focus.

It used to take a day and two horses pulling
through the scent of ox eyes, cockle burrs and horse breath,
to get to Anton Chico. That's what they got
for iron tires and draft animals.

They still carried Coronado's 500 year old phobia,
riding onto the face of that vast, blank negative:
believing in the saints, half looking for old markers.

Over by the church cornerstone, someone's
chapped lips and deeply calloused hands,
in one tobacco breath praise the abundance and long hours,
of times when men cut a thousand fence posts a day,
thankful they could pull at the brittle earth for *lajas*,
the local stone, then lay spent
like the blackened brass of buffalo guns.

MI TIERRA

What would I give you my *tierra*
to watch you sweep
the hair from your morning face
standing paralyzed
tight in the golden aperture
of your iris.

What would I give you
under the New Mexican sun
to nap on the moss side of canyons,
lie on life, quietly enduring,
awaiting the next great catastrophe.

She laughs at me
who never strayed
beyond the rim of God's
blue inverted bowl.

She says I go like a worried Spaniard
approaching the edge of the world.
My mother's voice asks if I'm afraid of America;
keeping my place
with stakes on boundless prairies.

The crone's kiss that comes from the lichen
tells me Mother Earth loves me
even as she grinds my bones with her gravity.

Now, ice that cracks away from her face
reveals the map of where we buried our troubles.
They come up suddenly, embarrass us,
like Loren Eisley's dandelions
with the same purpose as the space shuttle
surviving the napalm of re-entry.

Are these the flowers that make me dream?
Is my task to show we suffered here?

WALKING SOUTH

Me, I'm going to walk south
and pace it so I get
to Tierra Del Fuego in a hundred years.

I will kiss Sacajawea goodbye,
say hello to Mangas Coloradas,
read the lines on stern Geronimo's face—
invite him to plant flowers at Sand Creek,
eat whole coffee beans, handfuls of flour
to remember Bosque Redondo.

Wearing my Chicano ghost shirt
I'll walk in Cuahutemoc's empty shoes
smuggling out the songs of Victor Jara,
about political body parts,
boxes of toes from run-aways,
boxes of hands, jars of pickled
kidneys, and confiscated corneas,
eyes of witness, tongue of snitch
ears of more,
and skulls of the rest.

Kindly, he'll see me out the south causeway
on the way to Xochicalco,
on the way to Monte Alban,
on the way to La Venta,
on the way to Usumacinta's
mass graves in the jungle.

NELSON

Tired, still looking the murderous brute in the eye,
Nelson hung on only to help
with his own housekeeping;
putting away the well-burnished tools
of statesmanship.

How must it have been
your tongue, your teeth gagging
on someone else's flag?
How must it have felt, the itch
across your palms–to pound the freedom drum?

The mantle of your endurance
caped over the red earth of your country
made me turn to the man
who muttered: "Twenty seven years."
It made me say: "You've got it wrong friend,
no one gets 27 years for writing
his thoughts on toilet paper."

I'm glad you came in my time,
like Comet Kahoutek.
The world seldom gives us its face,
it shrugs, looms indifferent.
You gave us yours on the way
to the presidency, riding in back
of a battered Toyota.

What else could we do with two comets
and the taste of liberty?

In America

In America, food is a shrimp without a head,
manicured tidbits, colored balloons and tap water.

In America hunger is a petroglyph quail
that ran through the mind of an artist.

In America hunger is at noon, with white
sheets on the clothesline, my mother
and Patti Page singing Mockingbird Hill.

In America the hottest spot under the sun
is a beet field with Rainbow Bread,
a can with four sardines and *cuatro compañeros*.

Hunger is the klinkity klink of the fork with
a speared chunk of tortilla, round and
round the bottom of the peanut butter jar.

In America it was Quail Girl's sisters
in the year one thousand who
gave us the original cooking show,
ground out a likeness of their womanhood,
bashing with a phallic pestle 'til the sandstone
gave way, one grain per month.

In America, he stole whole steers, but
it was a midnight snack
that felled Billy the Kid.
Hunger.

DOORWAY

How many people have you seen
standing in a doorway like that girl
S-curved, thumb-on-toothbrush
enshrined sun-gilded Madonna.

The fifth grade door to the dentist—
behind that one, your lip turns to liver,
and you never forget burnt horn.

The door's voice groans across the *Zocalo*,
lets in the smog and smell of street tortillas.
They follow you to where golden candles light up
a tiny saint standing in a doorway.

There was no door on that Soviet sub
where men wrote their last thoughts standing.pitch.black.neck.
deep.cold.water.
"They'll come and get us."

Slam the door in anger, old custom,
kid slams it to punctuate the day.
Man slams a period walking out.
A bureaucrat slams his big black book
like a door on a submarine.

There is no door like the door to the moon:
El puerto de luna, PDL, even the letters lock.
Tamayo's Sandia in the sky,
watermelon rind in the sky.

No One Got Rich

No one got rich watching
Sombra and me fall in love
under Richard's back-from-Nam cross.
No one got rich when speaking *puro Chicano*.
Money Pacheco looking straight
at my first grade face, said through his big teeth,
"There used to be a Superman,
Pero lo mataron con una 'Tomic Bamb.'"
But they killed him with an atomic bomb.
Must've been about the time
of Ginsberg's Howl he heard this.

It's the beat of these lines,
I can't get enough of it–
wore the grooves off the record
like sugar cane.
I hold this song in my mouth
pulling on the taste of it–
Bob James's Women of Ireland:
I can't get enough of this–
wore the grooves off the record
like sugar cane.
I hold this song in my mouth
pulling on the taste of it
like the widow pulls the juices of her prey,
like the smoker pulls for the nicotine fix.
I can't get enough of this–
wore the grooves off the record
like sugar cane.
I can't get enough of this.

Ocean Poem, To Eliseo and Emmy

The tumbling waves are salty
with all the tears of humanity,
the bitter water no one wants
to talk about is there,
ready to crystallize.
The salary of Roman armies is there,
the sweat of Vikings,
the saline pillars of those who looked back.
Set your compass:
look ahead,
look ahead.

7TH SYMPHONY ON A RAINY DAY

Let's go wind ourselves
around the pole of flaccid living,
so weak that white hairs grow on our warts,
having become mutts with a checkbook;
spiting ourselves, giving
away those grimy prayers–
the ones we squandered–
the ones that Shostakovich phrased
so you could hear the rubble invoke
the unforgetable smoldering mattress.

It used to sicken me, worrying that our species
would dwindle to nothing but a blackened novena.

Now, I hope it happens soon–the coming of the savior,
bringing back each dog I've seen,
suffering square in the middle
of a bald lawn, licked clean as the kitchen
pots at Auschwitz. Choking on a chain.
It could be Jesus in a sleet–frozen coat–
no one caring–and each doe, a tragic, smiling
Madonna-of-the-Cadillac hood ornament.
Oh how we need those prayers.

WINDY DAY IN PDL

On a windy day in PDL
I got tired the way that *latón* got tired.
The wind pushed it and
pulled all during the *Cuaresma*.
Somebody's prayers couldn't
soothe the restless flapping.

P'aca y p'aya y p'aca y p'aya, all day.
And the place where it was attached
became so bitter and hardened,
that the bond gave way.
And it was a windy day at *Cuaresma*
when that *latón* let go.
It didn't care–tired
of going p'aca y p'aya y p'aca y p'aya all day.
It let go when another prayer and a gust of wind
pushed it into the mesquites behind the church,
and someone nailed it to the chicken coop.

CHAVEZ

We stood
like two wet colts at the starting line.
Born the same day, same year, same month.
I'd never heard my mother so formal say: "*Incate.*"
Got the blessing and went off just like that.
Nobody kneels in the dirt these days and
Trailways doesn't run any more Okies or
New Mexicans past a moon-lit million Saguaros.
Neither did we save the notes we passed
to the girls we lost at Tehachapi.
Four greasy days and heavy eyeglasses
made me learn to wiggle my ears
just in time to hear "Fresno, thirty minutes."

Because we spoke English, we got to sit
in the cool after-shave air of his truck.
The drama of the green Deere tractor
and tomato field theater of the poor
was real life. That oil pan plug, rattling to
the vibration of the times, came unscrewed.
It was real life in summer of 1966.
We all look back the way you did that day,
skillfully plowing the delicate, modified tomatoes
'til you dug up someone else's problem.

Milepost 6 read 1 more mile to payday when
the shirtless one yelled "Goddamned Portagees!"
Any hot day on a blacktop road
sends me–yellow paycheck in hand–
recalling how you stuffed the guy's face in the hot sand.
All it took was a chicken wing and a half nelson.
Sweet grapes for the conqueror.

We've traveled far but no plow can
cover our work or our memory.
If we could but cover our cares,
solving them as we did in the carnival glassware booth;
beat 'em at their own game with spit and dimes.

Having trudged the endless beet fields
as one might the Steppes of Marco Polo,
we came home–suitcase full of goblets,
like spices from the west, Rat Fink tee shirts,
surfer crosses, a rumpled City Lights copy of Candy
and every top ten song that ever flew out a transistor radio.

BILL'S PLACE

Hooo in front of Bill's Place
it was all those black heels tucked
back up against the wall, trying to look
like urban aborigines lying in wait;
dreaming, questing and looking
like Coronado on that
hot day crossing the Pecos.

The *pachucada* acutely listened
to the kid who pointed things out
with his lower lip– "*asina.*"
The indifferent wall includes the vato
with the bad hand, includes
El Pinto–a map of Texas speaks
from his face, in front of Bill's Place.

We dreamed in front of everybody
against the white wall, tending the gossip.
Dad comes home early morning
talking about the head-on near Pastura
amid the aroma of frying salt pork.
"Esque 90 miles an owwerr"?

After Mass Utsi and I go see
in the wreckage, among the seat springs,
plainly painted with blood,
little pieces of meat a kid touched
with a stick that bright Sunday.
Talked for days in front of Bill's Place.

One day in Autumn the sun's richness
irradiated the after-school arena
where two disheveled girls
cat-clawed each other in
an epic struggle in back of Bill's Place.

There was the nattily dressed one
on baby moons and chromed rims
who cruised regularly, pushing along
in his elder-auto. Eeeasing over the bump
in his elder-auto, in front of Bill's Place.

On that sidewalk stood the kid
who dreamed the whole town
stamped the brackish ground in sync
and brought back the buffalo.
Beautiful bison invented Route 66,
on the look-out for the red-mouthed wolf,
running from the Folsom dreads.
Following the ice-gouged earth long ago,
they ran in front of Bill's Place.

January, sunning on that wall
we dreamed in front of everybody.
Candy wrappers swirled, peanut bags
hung in the lee evoking grade school,
when we pulled the cellophane apart
to lick the oily salt the way cavemen
cracked bones for marrow.

In a conversation Amelia asks the
Rivera kid a dietary question about breakfast.
"Yes',' he said with pomaded hair,
"a cup of coffee and a cigarette."
Toasted and buttered?
Timed just right, the screen door
slammed a lot in front of Bill's Place.

Hooo we could've hung on that corner
for an entire life, watching Bill by the
meat scale–slicing Bologna and cheese,
a lifetime of slices slathered
with the butter of that golden age,
that makes us ache to go back
and spend a little time,
in front of Bill's Place.

THE MERCANTILE

Up the street, where the parade always
turned the corner the elders preferred,
stood the old bent Poseidon, salt on his face
and the grandmothers in black,
whispering the scent of crushed geraniums.

Below the idle pigeons and the whitewashed pulley,
the winos handing us our humility
through the vent, sleep it off in the coolness
under the beams.

When your eyes adjust, barn-red
letters say: Moise Brothers Mercantile.
Old commerce, the smell of coarse rope,
cattle cake and lanolin. The thick planks
of the place, strewn with ledger paper:
"1926, pocketknife, fifty pounds
Flour, 1 box 45/70s."

You could almost follow the wagon back
past Agua Negra, past the cross on the mesa,
looking back through the five o'clock light
that could have been Egypt,
remembering how little our part of the world was.

And do you remember the grassy bosom
of the golden hour? Feeling alive, we've all seen
the long shadows of the golden hour,
tasted the earth butter of the golden hour.
How beautiful and lulling,
her arched neck craned and kissable
out there on Fort Sumner Road,
each afternoon holding life and death
in the clam shell of her hands.

Rusty Fence at Agua Negra

The plate says "1931," a faint Hopi sun,
more rust than yellow, hangs on a man-made thorn—
raw material for a crown or shrapnel
from Verdun or dogtags forged
by thunder at Omaha Beach.
Even here, as the youngest waited
for the hen to cackle the day's last egg,
was heard the animal wail from such bloodied places.
Even here! that thunder fell like dust
into the folds of his overalls,
snagged like burrs in her socks,
caught like *masa* beneath her nails:
heard over the noise of chain and harness,
between chomps of watermelon rind.
Heard like dirt-clods on a hollow box.

Fewer wires bring the music back to town.
Now, they carry the little yellow songs
no one wants to hear. "Dear sir, we regret . . ."
We are losing the need for this old strand
and the wild flowers that come.

24

That strand needs hail and lightning,
needs Bing Crosby and Jimi Hendrix.
It needs a gloved hand and a juniper, now and then
to run through, needs the wispy wet bark, pungent
with the spice of rain.
It needs the cold, washed stinkbugs
and the bones buried in that bank
where tiny red flowers narrate
the vernal message one can read
through the delicate
cellophane wings of the dragonfly.

I KNOW A ROAD

I know a road you can cruise
at the pace of drunken earthworms
with a *quartillo* and a *leño*.
Out here, truth, Tomas can tell you,
pops like a seed,
spills like innards in
an upside-down sheep.

I know a road lined with the labor
of my ancestors. They never spoke
of the bruising task by which they came.
With their steady words–
I hope from this roadside–
they will speak well of me, hoe in hand,
bent from the waist, torqued at the wrist.

A black road we all know
ends where *Borica* began long ago.
It disappears around a curve
we are not allowed to see the end of.
It goes as far as carried on
the voice of *Zinzontles* in the *mesquital*
and the thirsty doves that come on Sunday.

Few have stepped here since
someone came from the albumin of the sea,
gathered ten stones in a circle
and sang to the dawn.
Climb the *cerro!* mingle the love we have
for the gray skirt of the impending storm
and the gift beneath the loam.

BLACK STONE FAMILY

That story book had satin ribbons
that split the pages.
From there came the little girl
who threw dirt in the bean pot
and
Joseph's coat of all colors,
always–the cruel desert and
the giant they threw rocks at.
Who kept the trophy stone? like
the man at the county fair
who kept the silver dollar
with the bullet hole.
The morals that pressed the linoleum
flowers into our little knees still hold me.

The ocean with the smell of dissolved
rock on its breath still wets your feet on the shore.
Its song bids us follow the tumbled pebbles
that move an inch for each ten thousand years.
Their black hardness endures like human nature
until something harder comes.

Out of the toy box,
Jesus played with you.
Cain picked up your bigger brother.
David chose a one pounder and
slung it at the giant.
Which of you was hefted by those without sin?
Were your black sisters at the stoning?
Who was there when Jericho crumbled?
In Ecclesiastes–gathered or flung–
and elsewhere chased away the dog
tending to Lazarus by the gates after
we are done with our stockpile.

Vaughn, New Mexico, 1943

If I wrote this in rhyme, the symmetry would
create fault lines and crack the spell.

This requires one leafless tree,
a train yard, the *llano*
and an odd year like 1943.

Nothing there resembles the starved
and the old, contemplating eating
their European horse
as the trains come in.

My mother, pretty as a prairie rose
doing her part, takes orders
for roast beef, wards off the passes
with gorgeous teeth.

Her accent springs word to word
coffee, toast, and feed the black
soldiers ushered into the kitchen.

In the year when water froze
in the apartment bucket
she slept, bone tired
as Leningrad, too far away to be heard,
cooked sawdust and linseed oil
and pretended it was bread and butter.

MISA

Remember the *Boletin*,
the gessoed saints and angels;
the whisper of stockings
leaving the confessional.
The wind outside moans:
"tuuu," and sifts dust through
the cracks in our porcelain.

They pray, they remember the ache,
a lifetime of confessions to get it right.
Above the squeaky stairs to the choir
something hovers like canvas.

Oh bring us back from the milk of amnesia,
from the opacity of mortal sin.
With this purple shroud and the Latin Mass,
with this incense bring us back
to the sisterhood of Doña Petra and Doña Irenez.

I squeeze this pen like a nipple
that it would say more:
How they cared for each other;
doted over their geraniums,
held their solemn Lenten exchange
of simple food for decades.
How one held the yellowing hand of the other
and seanced the chemo of absolution.

When no one gave them a ride
they walked–through stinging wind
or meadow larks, walked–
Petra in her good shoes

sturdy heart and obdurate creed.
Irenez with her bandana, Cat Woman glasses
polka-dot dresses, all the same.

They walked and thus crossed paths
with the unsung nation I wish
my blood was made of.

When the world got up that cold Sunday
few heard the bells and
paced right past the bar at Pastura.
In from the damp Savannahs!
Up from the cattails!
In their steaming shagginess–
sated on red meat–come the rulers of North America.
No paradise gained or lost here,
the ravaged and cracked stubs of fingers
hunt and gather tules for insulation, and knowledge
to find the lowest rib and the soft spot.
They left their songs by the hearth,
and finely flaked cutlery
strewn from Tierra del Fuego to Florida.
We found advice in their charcoal:
"Read your dogs."

Doña Petra gets up, feels the air,
remembering the deal they'd struck
she lets the dogs in and prays for Lazarus.
Who said what to make their faith
so like the stonemason's wall?
"Read the Good Book."

Oh precious *Librito de Rezar*, like a tired sparrow
bearing news, lies spent in someone's hand.
A palm leaf marks the page saying:

"Jesus falls the first time by the Comet Drive-In."
Irenez spoke and someone ran for water–
found the spring in the front row at the theater
where you cannot sit,
by the silver screen, now showing
Antonio Aguilar and coming soon Brando and Monroe.
Ave Maria q' 'tas en los cielos
Bells sound the call to Mass.

By the newspaper office, He falls the second time;
the headline read: "*ya crucificaron a un bandido.*"
The bells peal halfway to Puerto–*ven, ven, ven.*
Calling past the homely stunted corn,
calling past the pumpkins and chile verde.
calling to the stonemason, Juan Largo and Saturnino;
all took turns shouldering the cross
when no one else would get involved.

Someone in a red shawl–looked like Ira Hayes–
ran for help. He knew this man–seen him at Iwo Jima–
he had sat under the bridge rolling smokes
while Jesus strummed. Then soldiers
crowned him with mesquite, took his bike
as Juan Largo removed his work boots
gave them to him; Doña Amada
wiped his face with a polyester rag.

Several got rich when the earth cried
and no one laughed when they brought the last
of the cold mineralized water,
heavy with tears and unwanted memory.
Saturnino washed his bloody knees, waved away the flies,
squeezed pink water from a rag.

Never forget this day said Doña Petra,
Pray for rain, for the dead.
In cottonwood shade wet your faces
with the river John Baptist crossed.
Step in the mud of cliff swallows and receive your name.
Remember the thirsty doves–it wasn't their fault
Jesus forgave them.
But the soldiers–the scourge of soldiers–
behind the barbershop, avoiding crowd control duty,
roll the dice for his robe.

All he wanted could've filled a single *bote de diez*.
His simple shoes filled by simple feet.
And Doña Petra's fondest memory: her
children among the linoleum flowers,
overruns the threshold of my heart.
Saturnino, hung over, his work worn soul
plaquened thick with his own dark sin,
apologizes for the broken wine bottles,
hefts the weight of two railroad ties,
looks down the remaining road.
The sale is on at Wal-Mart, robes, purple, Dacron:
where is their crystal cathedral now?

PECOS

When the *Sangre de Cristo* slows
to a red meander,
clotted to a domesticated pace,
follow it out. Accept the mud of baptism;
live with the accords of its delta, like the *chile verde*.
Be thankful it comes to this quiet place,
that it releases its mongrel fertile load like these
granule words of loam and loess and rock flour,
that it drops them far from the cold and crystal roar and fury,
urged to cleave the rhombic blocks,
its parents standing
on the alpine toes of Christ,
where the common granite told the trout
how to paint itself and blend into your bosom.

STEP IN THE MUD

Step in the sunlit mud of cliff swallows.
Wet your head with this water.
Smell the wine of the Russian olive.
Fill your hands with the silt that comes
of all this restless running.

Each leaf that moulders,
with each fish papered between
the delicate layers
on which is printed the unedited story
of all things down to the last
settling speck of quartz and iron
that slows and stops,
adding its little soul
to the unlit space.

SAID MOOSE TO ME

Said Moose to me
"Why do you keep running into the subject
each time you take a walk?
Is this about the time you made an animal suffer?
I'll go in his place;
you don't even remember his name.
You could've euthanized him,
and that big word would've paid the bill.
You could've given someone else the responsibility
and so you did.
You could've shooed the thirsty animal
and his flies, his stench and his maggots.
Ignored him like the dry mouths at Calvary.
So you turned your back on him
and the next day he was dead."

Why is the sheep black, the goat Judas and you unlucky?
I've been told someone's god sends defective,
injured spies for his running bet;
the big lark is to see how each is treated.
That patient black cat waiting by the road
understood: with every meal comes a little death;
remembered his own run-ins; his
blackness bears the rasp of a Miles Davis,
the coolness of his lip.

Moose came to my tired porch.
Neither knew who'd go first–we didn't care
the year we burned every stick
the apple tree could spare.
When I packed to leave that white house,
an old can of mackerel in the basement
brought back your yellow eyes.

THINGS I FOUND IN THE GARAGE

I love the Codetalkers' fat iron fish,
and something like reverence
welled up recalling when my mother said "Korea"
as she wrapped the ribbon candy
before my little eyes.

I could tell you about Iwo Jima
at age six. When the soldiers
raised the flag, you could see
the hard and unwashed men and
the hands of all America.

Smelling the coppery sweat,
you could see in the bronze
the thick veins like the ones
on back of my father's hands.

And the hands of Ira Hayes
help out hoping he might
bring water to his people.
I found the story in my
father's trunk, how he died.

I have this frazzled scrap that says,
with much less resources
the *Zapatistas* pray the rosary
with a belt full of cartridges
as they shoulder the burden–again.

What would Ike say
to *Commandante* Marcos
as one more time, they
are recruited by their dreams,
because the price of coffee
continues to be the same as
a shrug at the local bistro?

Because He Could Not Swim

Because he could not swim,
we traced a muddy stream to a geographic lesson.
Because his drowning shoe could not be saved
I know where to find the Mexican gulf.
One million years later,
that neoprene soul will lie in a vast delta
next to Ferlingetti's ballpoint pen.

Because he could not swim
we got a whipping. The whup
of a salt cedar switch
did not deter the sting of knowledge.
Come to think of it, neither could
those daily thumps from Miss Thompson's
fat eraser buy a kid's mind
with the strange currency of English.

Because he could not swim,
and because he could not say it,
he could not teach us much with
an angry heartless branch hastily cut
from the *bosque* of fatherhood.

Because he could not swim,
all this rang in his ears a long time.

STANDARD, OPEN ALL NIGHT

It's still there, the place by the road where you
and Tom Joad stood out in the coolness of 3 a.m.
amid the cottonwood smell
of the river air the big semis rush through.
You wave at the Navajos, Fergusson-Steers
and the Illinois-California-Express. If they
stopped being your dream, it never showed.

While your cigarette burned another notch
in the post hoisting the chain link,
the red neon buzzed its low voltage
approval, even when the crying priest
gave you his dog.

And there were nights when it
was merely the local boys twisting
to Green Onions in those
impeccable lime-green pants
out on the driveway.

Under the game lights I felt your unease
through the thick helmet on
football night as you stood by me
on neoprene soles, in khakis
and your keyring. I found out
you walked all the way back to town.

I found out you whispered to the old barber
in the utter luxury of pride,
in the molasses of it:
"Yep, two kids in college,"
even when nothing was left over–
"*Ni pa' los Luckies.*"

You could've been Jesus with a tire gauge,
you could've been Joseph,
the patron saint of snow chains,
cursing the soggy money.

I found out how you kept
bringing your teeth home in
your shirt pocket, one by one,
and now I understand . . .
all you sacrificed
made those gaps which
I can only fill with
love yous and I thank yous.

HUGGING 101

When I hugged my dad,
When I knew those sagging
Vertebrae were back there,
When it became okay to embrace,
After he realized, "Must come
With education," and
Now that it's done
And has been brought home
Like the record albums
That made him hum Scarborough Fair
While shaving over that hot basin,
He might as well.

And so it was
We stood in the spring night
Of 1978, my pop ever with
His keyring and khakis
And me in my college shorts,
Moths flying all over
The red rancho neon.
–I went first–

You Don't Know Me Ray Charles

The lines left out of this poem
are children of even keel,
not worried about being favorites.
Smiling in the little pictures,
we waited patiently under
a great army overcoat and old brass
in a trunk,
while Sputnik made the rounds and
he collected our grade school photos.

Down at the gas station,
awaiting my next assignment,
florescent tubes glowed to razz
those songs with static as a lone clarinet
blowing "Stranger On the Shore"
bleated way into the night.

Next up, Ray Charles gives his hand to me
warm as that wooden radio.

As I mopped the lube-room floor
the swell of those orchestral strings scrubbed my soul.
I watched Dad clomp across to answer the phone.
"Starley's Standard" he booms–
all military police . . . yet still unequipped
to speak that jagged language.
Those shards got in his way as some Tejano
almost made him lose his temper one night
when a volatile, six foot declaration splashed the driveway:
"I ain't payin' for what that kid spilled."
He was Joe the diplomat; in fountain ink signed his name
with the flair of an old president,
even on the note in the warm paper bag
carrying onion and coffee memory.

That red, white and blue chevron
and the Del Rey Cafe–long gone–
were the lonely sentinels of that golden place
few carry the keys to.

ELISEO–GONE TO THE LIGHT

I was told it was you they saw
running the ridge and gliding
like a blue swallow
across Quail Girl Canyon,
to join those who have gone to the light.

You have given back
the small white smudge
that was your smile.
Given back
a handful of minerals–the sum total,
enough for one arrow to
pierce us all in the heart that so loved you;
enough iron for three nails and the void that was left.

We release you–
with a glad sigh–
to go with the dandelions
that they may lead you
to the peace you could not find on this earth.

MIGUELITO'S THREE BLACK ROCKS

Vast prairie space and human indifference
shield a secret here older than statehood.
Only those stones mark praise for the lonely
Franciscanos–up ahead–walking point
with the Moor, to the very edge of earth.

Having stepped through the barbed wire
into a time when raiding was honorable,
my father stood in the tall wet grass
tuned in to the message of warbling larks
as the slot of early dawn waited for a dime.
"Ummhumm" he pronounced.
"They say at sunset Coronado clanked through here
with fifty bleating sheep.
They say out here, expressing a look as flat as this place,
Abuelo Miguelito sang like Comanches,
laughed at the *Rinches* with his Athabascan teeth
slaked white by the lime in his tortillas."

They say amid these standing stones that keep the page,
Miguelito counted his rounds, ate *carne seca*,
watching the blunt slugs pit the dark rock.

When foreign law came to erase both rocks and men,
even hopeless renegades became friends.
That winter, the whispering snow on the *llano*
came to lie like shawls on meager shoulders
every bit like Rodin's Burghers of Calais.
And the mute stones–like Black Robes–
heard their last confession and gave it to the wind.

In his memory, my father sings over the shaving basin
the same guiltless Miguelito songs:
"Come closer native child and rest
while I count the fortune in this pouch."
A hundred and five years later,
through the peep sight on this old Henry,
you can see them—getting away.

Soldados De La Luna

"The soldiers of the moon are coming!"
cried Tia Florinda, in the days before The Enquirer.
"They leave oil spots where they been standing."
We second graders tried to imagine
someone so much like us.

She probably concluded the greasy smudge we leave behind
darkens the earth with human oil.
The same ooze come from our pores asks how many kisses
to wear out the Blarney Stone? It asks who
wore out the steps of great cathedrals?
The thinned pavers of Roman roads?
Who wore out the well-known spot on the Buddha?

Florinda knew about Little Richard.
That and the sound of her gum snapping
made her gush like a teenager listening
to Richard gulp air as he reached
for that note in praise of Lucille.

She married Cristino who married the whisk broom
that cleaned the friendly yellow bus.
I saw that happy man at four in the morning,
heard the whisk whisk and the raspy
ionospheric voice from Juarez say
"Diez mil watts de potencia!"

When he poked the raging stove and dawn
came in on a shower of stars,
that Mariache yell came like a banner.
The potency of such music lingers like his question,
still asking me—"*Eres valiente?*"
"*Are you brave?*"

PAINTBRUSH

It comes to me like the plastic
Madonna-in-the-dark why
Brother Alfred loves the
fields of paintbrush:
they soften the carpal tunnel
of an over-strained soul,
their sweetened stamens, burnt
orange, surround the *Campo Santo*.

I'll see your Indian paintbrush
and raise you the music
of the wildwood flower
coming through the dust
from that sky-blue pick-up.

The patient *Campo Santo* loves those back
who tried to weigh a soul.
How can you weigh the scent
of a giant brown quart
of beer as it evanesced out
of that '32 Willys?
Who would know that lightness?
Unhefted except by
that little heart in the back seat,
guarded by two GIs–khaki
sleeves rolled up–who
still obey my shrunken grandfather;
drive out to Johnson's farm after the rain,
still return with the richest milk in the world.

PURO

Quiet as a moth
in Milagro he listens to the radio
with the ten-pound battery.
In the dark in 1959 Abuelo Salinas's
angry cigar flares up with each
roar of the Cuban crowd
far away from the island.

As they were all lined up and shot
in black and white before the world,
each stern pull on that cigar
drew out the wrath to meet
the moment four million tons
of sugar could not sweeten.

The leaves on his peach tree
whisper like nuns at prayer,
lisping some Novena to the
disemboweled saints.

This memory is soft as sheepskin
under the sewing machine
the year that revolution
reached clean into cattle country.

AGUA FOR DELFINIA

She said: I've never met my soul
I hope someday to meet it.
Never fall to sleep with thirst,
should your soul get up to drink,
your cat might catch and eat it.

Smelling the soap tub
and old meat hanging,
you see a lot eating by lantern;
necessity defining faces burnt
from looking up, etched
by the undiluted acid of worry.

The one-armed *Santo* overlooking
the tepid waterhole, works
in greater cycles than ourselves.

I see the sisters moisten
her lips with a sponge.

So close to the dolphins,
she carried her saline surname.

She lived and died thirsty,
lived and died eating by lantern
lived and died rolling her own
lived and died in one language
lived and died listening for thunder
lived and died without malice
tending her creamy yuccas
white as the parched *caliche*.

TAPS FOR US

With the unconditional love of children
I still hold dear the breath of the meadow
that carries the mixed emotion
of the larks and the sound of taps
coming from Saint Joseph cemetery.

Slams the locker in the high school hall,
scrapes the crutch on the janitor's floor,
everybody knows the etched, black
granite of our generation.

Everybody knows the taste
of the warm tarmac on the soldier's lips,
the fading, pearly, milk-fed smile,
the frazzled pompoms they put away in '67.

Replete with the warble of redwing blackbirds
and the signature of Russian olive,
everyone returns lulled by the blooms of the *yucca*—
white as an altarcloth—new Lotus for old sirens,
fit for that peaceful place we haven't found.

Lately, the music we wrote to wander the
world by—still tasting of tarmac—
fades to a strong but minor key.

SUMMER READING

No matter the summer sun on the tin roof.
Mrs. York's Lily-of-the-Valley scent
stuck to the air conditioned books
that sent us to Hemingway's house
to pick up the read and white pieces of stories:

there's one about Spencer Tracy holding on
to that string pulling him as he salts
his fish with seawater,
pulling me along that summer on my stomach,
eyes two feet from the floor.

The faint taste of old iced tea
as I tried to read On the Origin of Species
is all that remains of seventh grade.

PRUDENCE

I can't remember when we noticed
he was different, an adult who wore spats.
Maybe through that heavy darkroom camera.
Maybe when the black and white image loomed;
caught mid-stride: gaunt sailor in the tray
at midnight, like his stories.

When he topped the stony ridge with a violin case,
something told me the green in his eye
came from copper bracelets.

With an apothecary of old Spanish words
he named parts in a box of old clocks.
I got by his vicious dogs,
I saw his gun collection,
I learned grooves from lands and
understood how rivets worked.

Ringing from the dark across the road
his eight bells made me dwell on rumors
about his crystal ball at night,
about how that tipped hat in daylight
shaded the genius of a Cerevantes.

He talked to himself with hand signs,
while others got his jade gaze.
Scuffing by on horseshoe taps that
kept time for him and Bernabé
strumming down at the *Salita*.

He knew under Don Asencion's mattress
lay hidden the handwritten hymnals
done in stubby pencil–two hundred years
of *Penitente* music–he had no need of.

EDITH

Thanks to Mrs. Greves in her corset
I am the half couplet in the pollinated sunlight
loving the full-lipped kiss of these great rocks;
stations of the cross where I stand
and kneel. To this day I have carried
your red dust like the Baptist carried Jesus;
looking up past Orion all those nights,
dreaming of the muddy tea
in drips off the whiskered fish.
None of this is in vain–
I have carried you better than most,
quietly, *penitente* style.

If the unborn had walked here
I'd have shushed them to hear
the canyon wren's count:
one-two-three-four-five-six-seven
Eight-nine-ten.

Sometimes lamenting the sum
of my unbegotten children
a great white thunderhead
comes to me
from some holy sadness.

Sometimes when my heart skips a beat
it is given to the little ones in Limbo.
The quiet heartaches stand
light as a wasp poised to inflict
a pain the size of an anvil.

I have stories still to tell:
about the child who drowned in the Nile,
about Danny on the Pecos,
about Archie standing with the quiet
moths and the army-green bass.
All those souls will tangle in a weir of salt cedar twigs
as they silt their way to the sea.

JOHNNY BARAÑA AT THE RACK AND CUE

A bunch of Chicanos in front of *El Pool*
made a wish out into the street where the *bachas* lay
hoping Marilyn Monroe might arrive
in her golden airplane
as smoke curled up like an oracle,
back when *Guero* sang acapella
and little sister kept time on the washtub.
This was years ago you see,

when I envied the shine boys their income,

when the diver's mask in the drugstore window
went for four ninety nine,

when the cracked bell on the half
rang true across that cool marble slab at the bank,

when Johnny Bee still spun around the light pole
like West Side Story, longing for the first taste of the day.
I never looked too close,
or knew his complicated feelings.
He lived with Grandma
who knocked back at the Jehovah's Witnesses;
chased away the vacuum cleaner salesman
who tried to sell her one to clean her dirt floors.
We knew Johnny was down to his last dress pants,
the black ones, still good after Sister School.
We knew each scuff on his shoes,
knew he lived on the edge, completing the list
of pearl divers at the Club Cafe.

SUMMER OF '61

Under Doña Elogaria's evening porch
Jesus gets down off his bike,
listens quietly to the cleaning lady,
holds her poor chapped hands as three
Bull Durhams glow to become the Trinity.

Then something wafting in the hand-rolled smoke
caused Joe the Butcher to say
from that community canopy:
"No, I think they nailed him through
that part of the wrist where the
two forearm bones come together.
It would have held better."
He had hung meat so long
that no one argued.

OVERHEARD THROUGH THE SCREEN DOOR

When he came back,
it was overheard through the screen door
across the street where Nita
was evicting ants with a fly swatter.

It was right there on that hard earth,
full of practice foxholes,
the worried lady–chili flecks in her teeth–
saw what made her say:
"Just back from Korea
he knelt here in the dirt,
in the middle of the road,
trying to swallow a rosary."

He came back–big brother slung
his duffle like half a corpse
down at the yellow depot . . . same color
as the Buick in the rough shed,
the faithful *lajas* holding up those sleek lines
two hues lighter than the enemy.

MAGUIN

That summer watching the tourist girls
across 66, with my towel on my shoulder,
someone with a paper hat told me
out by the barrel of french fry grease:

Before Maguin held that spatula
he held an M-16.

Before pulling an arm from
its socket in that mass grave,
Maguin put on his shoulder pads
like an ox putting on its bow.
I'd never seen cloth stiffened by human salt.

Before he was an iron lion walking point,
he was an iron train–matte black with purpose,
focused, standing like an Olmec David.

Before she let go of his hand, under the shade of Alamos,
his mother shared with him a Fort Sumner melon.
That, and her blessing will keep him all his days.

PECA

Peca, hard to kill as an old jackrabbit
was a powder man. He must've blown up
tons of rusted steel, bamboo and powdered paint
before getting his answer from
a new record album he couldn't quit humming.

I was there when he blew out his voice
way up on the mesa,
singing into the spring wind,
gone searching for a heart of gold
at the top of his lungs.

Suddenly the skinny kid with the Polaroids
crowed "Peca went to Vietnam–pa,pa,pa,pa pa!"
In one picture smiling, posing plain to see,
Peca's hand casually draped back in the bleachers
for a few seconds, then back to the jungle.
If the war had still been on
all these little men would fit in the tunnels;
they were the village manpower;
endeared like Peca, to the art of Neil Young.

Turning the corner with thirty people in it
somebody called it the death bus.
"Nam is man backwards" argued
the hippie, two houses down.
He'd seen nobody come for a week as
the mayor's AWOL son lay in the bathtub in summertime
'til the postman noticed the flies.

EL SNIQUE AT THE STICKERBOWL

Me and Utsi arrived here in a pinch of dust–
Arrived here pollinating *calabasitas* in a gust–
Arrived here rolled up in a cottonwood leaf
down by the banks of the *asequia*.

We came across the border one night
when we crept under the fence at Walker Field
to watch the Lions and Foxes.
The first *mojados* in America,
watching Veronica in purple and white,
pom poms untouchable: perfect.

TARDECITAS ALEGRES: HONORING WILLIAM PAD

Up and down the daub and stones
of *Los Jarros*, each industrious hand
knew the mix was one cement, two sand
or three flour, one *manteca*.
And fixed on this, the citizenry toiled.
"*Tardecitas Alegres!*" boomed the radio,
it was double nutrition day
and in a hot puff of summer air
came the smell of scorched tortillas
and green chile to the cadence of trowels,
metered to respect Jose Alfredo Jimenez
lamenting from his famous corner.
Every wooden radio crooned down
the dirt road lined with dish towels
and *señoras* feeding the clock.
Nearsighted chickens pecked the peelings,
while simmering potatoes floated in chile broth.

"Come to this side of the tracks"
bade the rebel from a sweaty tribe of
Road Devils, roaring down the dirt street
on stripped-down bikes motorized
by the Ace of Spades and one clothespin.

And what of those tongues red with Kool-Aid,
skinny mouth breathers, smelling of pee and bubble gum?
They're all gone–evanesced like moths at dawn;
left that little hill with as much mystery
as Chaco Canyon; forgot the neat piles
of *Jarreño* rocks, hub cap shields and
cardboard pterodactyl wings that said "Maytag."

71

With the rubble of old words and a good plumb line,
the *tortilla* makers and stone masons of Maquel's time
stacked their work to the hearty songs of *Tardecitas Alegres*.

GOATS ON THE CLOTHESLINE

Being polite, the neighbor in 1956 agreed with his theory:
Victor's goats had lined up on her clothesline
like some abacus, keeping a strange score.

In 1972, it might've been clothespins all in a row
that fooled his eyes the morning when
Don Leandro forgot his passion for *Rancheras*
and Muscatel. All the years
the goats had gotten in his way
except the night the town met.

While everybody swept the school principal's red carpet,
Leandro carried memory of the ice age,
bore the scars of ancient Tlatelolco–
the last jaguar, the last eagle fell there.
Suddenly recalling, he put on his Aztec face,
stern as Cuauhtémoc, wielding
justice with an obsidian stare.

Trespassing orderly lines on the hardwood gym,
it could've been a church he stepped into.
The crease in his Levis straight as crosshairs,
his blackened *Mata-Viboras* contrasting
with handfuls of silver, swept-back hair.
Those angular features pulled across
the leathered jaw of a Solomon
seemed to fill the room with courage.

Next time, whose Atlatl will sing through
the spring air in that gymnasium?
Someone said down at *El Vasito* Bar:
"They found the abandoned Jeep in El Paso."
It's been a while since that con-job and
I've not looked at a clothespin the same since.
Someone is keeping score . . .

WHERE IS THE BELL?

I didn't need permission to stand quietly at noon on the mesa
above Brush Dam to hear the 400 pound bronze voice
clear as Lucha Villa, coming from Saint Rose's tower 7 miles away.
Where is the bell, its throat
its tongue and groan and knotted rope?
Too many things have been clipped as if courage grew on a vine.
That voice was poured by real muscle;
of metal stained green by real sweat.
It hasn't tolled right since they took its vocabulary and the man
with the coke-bottle glasses; replaced them with that anemic
Quasimodo in a tin box.

It tolled right when that picture of
the entire asphyxiated family
ran on the front page.
Square in the hometown news
the mother and father in the foreground
completely blackened–betrayed by a few atoms.
The two kids never woke up for school.
This is what happens to the indolent
opined the newspaper man just finished calling
Reverend King "a sex-crazed nigger"
and now these darkened people.

It might as well've been he who chugged whiskey
and put his pinky under the wraparound chain on that well casing;
eleven thousand bucks for the first joint.
They partied for a month deciding who was next.

I still think of Saint Rose and that bell
and how many people have walked beneath it.
How many black rosaries on a cold night
when the windows cry with the condensed breath of people
and straight up the silk curl of smoke from the censor rises.

God did this for a reason and left behind her dark braids.
When they took the little boy's things from the school desk
he faded away, left a darkened space.
Let's waltz Matilda all the way to Porteluna
past Brother Richard's house
on down to the Coronado Bridge stamped 1957.
Waltz us all past the *morada*–
white walls marked with the contusions
of so many sins and contritions.
Past the *milpa* and the *asequia*
where even the darkened people
go following the voice of Lucha Villa.

OCOTE

Glimmering in the red horizon,
Venus hung in the cold still air John sniffed
as he stepped through the door.

That's it! he said, that's
the smoke that has followed us
since we left these four walls, so ordinary
a few drops of rain would dissolve them.

They ought to pass a law, he said, exhaling:
everybody burn *ocote*.
On these words, one by one,
our minds wafted away on the dreamy
gauze of that familiar smoke.

With *ocote* chips on our shoulder we went,
with dirt in our shoes we went.
We said to the whole country
with our eyes,
"It's paid for."
We went undissolved, like flint pebbles,
knowing and sometimes not,
returning to gawk joyously into
that small nest for clues to how we came
like the delirious Cretaceous,
turning the oxygen-rich pages.

This year, across the road,
stark as crows on *caliche*, I saw
Fernando, bent over further
than his front gate,
his teeth down to one yellowed fang.
I watched him shuffling back in
with three letters from the mailbox,
before he closed the sun-washed door.

MARTA

I asked: Mama why does the moon
have half a face?
"*Mal espiritu,*" she says,
came on the unlucky days–
some argument with the sun,
but She always wins in the end.

I hope Marta Perez won. She told me
how she walked all the way to Santa Ana,
good shoes in hand, past banana leaves,
past the black waters and pig wallows
out of the jungle, out of the little village,
past the test administrator's well-fed face.

In a voice thickened by *Salvadoreño* coffee
and science, gesturing like a man,
she told me: the quiet pastime from her porch
was guessing calibers of evening gunfire.
She told me in borrowed English:
"Een my cawntree I seen two
fight to the death! A *machetasos*. I saw
the winner plaster half his face back on–
like a sandwich–and fight all the way to victory."

SISNEROS'S GOAT

With the use of this opposable thumb,
the same one Rockefeller uses to count his money,
we got a ride with Mr. Sisneros in back of his truck.
The only companion was a brown eyed goat we
struck a conversation with.
We talked about professional vandalism,
the kind where they wore a tie on a Sunday,
to sand blast the inflamed colors of our mural.
Although we never got to argue with a Rockefeller
we painted our own version of the troubles,
offended the guy with the tie and the PhD.

In the cold rushing air and swirling hay stems,
we spot a rolling spray paint can—
then the broad white side of this goat.
I look back to my college days,
it wasn't so bad—psssss—peace sign!

Pay Per Curse

It was little brother John's
remarkable knack for finding
the rare chance in the neighborhood.
Fourth grade was for dropping
pebbles on that tin roof–like coins in a jukebox
that played the muttering drunk's stream of curses for fun.

A DUTCHMAN'S VIEW AT STAR AXIS SITE

After he was done observing the earth's wobble and
done catching his breath from the effort it took
to fathom having to wait 13 thousand years,
he was ready for something closer.
Thinking of the little Dutchboy
struggling to save his sealevel homeland
over-served by the rising tide,
he scanned the ancient arid seafloor of New Mexico.
As the squealing windmills all looked in the same direction,
pulling the precious sap from the ground while his
countrymen pushed the waves away,
he asked:
"Who owns all this?"
That house six miles away is the owner's.
It's been in the family since the 1600s.
You got rich on tulips and masterpieces.
He got rich driving cattle on a cold day.

No matter, we are all the same size,
the soot of one's life neat in a shoebox and
still room for one of Dad's Florsheims.
Maybe if you spread my remaining molecules
on this red mesa no one will see me trespass;
my dust maybe deter the vandals and assholes
and half a dozen "rightful owners."

He walks away thoughtful of the *Goras Blancas*
and their fencemender pliers; thinking of
the fences seen by Thoreau or Whitman.
The Dutchman sees under the baked bricks that cover
everything, glances off beyond the six-mile house
to the hill we all go under.

THE LONG PLACE

Out on the *llano* with pronghorns born on the run
the storm holds all the marbles.
Hands come out of the ground,
people find money in their food.
UFOs hover close enough to prickle hair.
Out there, Brother Mark swallowed
a burr with his venison,
rehydrated when it barbed his gullet,
way out there, too far to walk.

Two matchless comrades and Brother
John in a thin sweater can tell you what
sixteen degrees in the dark feels like.
These high plains are where everything learned in college
equals one thermal unit. Too far to walk.
John losing consciousness, he dreamed Mom
handing him a blanket, whispered:
"Hug men under the stars."

It's the small things make us suffer: a burr,
home canned pumpkin, a small stone
in the clutch housing–God's creations.
The Eskimos have a trick, folding
a sharpened gristle knife in a ball of fat.
In the warm maw of the polar bear
the nutritious stiletto springs open,
the bear begins to die.

See where the birds spice the sky
Like a pinch of black pepper.
It was there two brothers died from botulism:
too far to walk they counted the neuro-toxic stars.
What did they say to each other?
How would you carry a jar of that guilt?
I will always pray for them.

This long place tells the story of the fence rider
huddled under his saddle while his horse
is killed by baseball hail. It tells how the son of somebody
touched the fence that carried the blue lightning:
all those rusted, twisted, splices held,
carried that message pure, out of the sky.

SANTA

Coming over this hill, Santa is a cheerful
face in a basin filled with memory,
her people one degree from
where God's thumbprint put us.

Coming over this hill is Santa like a girlfriend,
the silk scarves of your air come like mesquite
tassels swiping across my face.

Coming over this hill, Puerto de Luna
I love your face–you gave
me memories and arrowhead dreams
where every thunderhead was a hopeful bloom.

Coming over this hill, Santa gives me five
special minutes with the lozenge of her amber solace,
where each day cracks like piñon between
the clean and sturdy molars of river stones.

Look at this sun-planished place!
Boulders appearing like a salt-lick
sculpted by the tongue of time, and over
there the flat *lajas* breathe a message
tucked beneath them, old as Indians.

Santa, I'm sorry I left you,
each time you see that I atone.
I try to locate my friends among the stones;
it's getting harder to find them
and there are more stones than before.
There's Jimmy-Joe now: the legend is
he could do Santa to Brush Dam in the time
it took the radio to play
The Ballad of the Green Berets.

Forever young now in a '57 Chevy,
him and Boo Boo, and Suz, eternally cool,
would say *"Esos vatos estan fast."*
Coming over this hill I see the Alamo.
It's all still here—the *sotanos*, the *Chopilotes*, *Brujas*,
and balls of fire and the black bridge,
enduring like Atlas.

Coming over this hill to Santa's mystery Main Street.
Somewhere, barbers neatly clip and dab another scalp,
extracting data better than the CIA.

Thanks to Spider who goes on with the show
where for two dimes
the Creature from the Black Lagoon
would come on Saturday.
Where Joe Romero's big steel mike
would ring out on Saturday night:
"Good evening ladies and gentlemen and
welcome to the Pecos Theater, tonight's
drowwing is for *onne hunnndred twenntee dow-lers*.
But first we need two judges, twooo judgesss."
And two would come up, and one would spin the hopper,
and fumble with the latch and reach inside
while the other held the clipboard, hopeful as a dinner plate.

And Joe would call out the name of some guy who'd
stayed one night at the Rancho Motor Lodge in 1959,
no matter that it was already 1966.
I never got called–but I get called still.

Coming over this hill, it's all still here.
Santa is a girl with a broken heart,
and all those secrets and memories
she breathed into the river and thought
were gone like Moses are snagged
in cottonwood brambles at Brush Dam.
If you want them back–you can always go there.

ACKNOWLEDGMENTS:

I would like to offer my thanks to my parents, Jose and Petra, and to my brothers and sisters for their love and support. Thanks to all my close friends. Thanks to Edith Greve, Juan Lopez, the coaches and the other inhabitants of Santa Rosa. Thanks to Dennis Held for his guidance on the manuscript, and thanks to all the women and children and animals that made the saga of this life. Special thanks to Sandy, my wife and patient editor who always reminded me: "Haz algo."